World Book's Learning Ladders

Jobs to Do

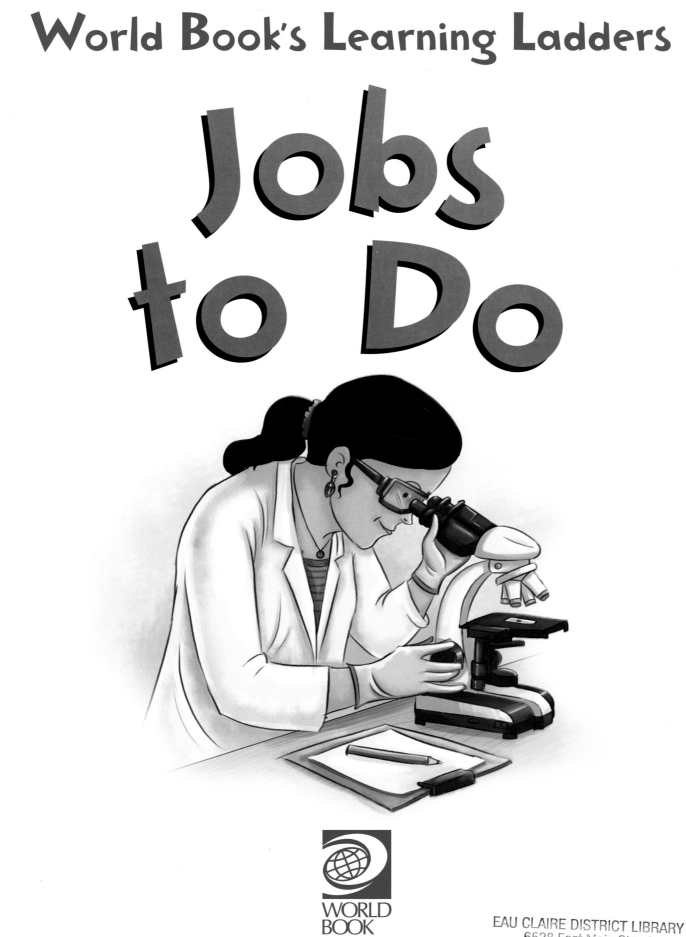

WORLD
BOOK

www.worldbook.com

World Book, Inc.
180 North LaSalle Street
Suite 900
Chicago, Illinois 60601
USA

For information about other World Book publications, visit our website at **www.worldbook.com** or call **1-800-WORLDBK (967-5325)**.

For information about sales to schools and libraries, call **1-800-975-3250 (United States); 1-800-837-5365 (Canada)**.

Library of Congress Cataloging-in-Publication Data for this volume has been applied for.

World Book's Learning Ladders
ISBN 978-0-7166-7945-5 (set, hc.)

Jobs to Do
ISBN 978-0-7166-7949-3 (hc.)

Also available as:
ISBN 978-0-7166-7959-2 (e-book)

Printed in China by Shenzhen Wing King Tong Paper Products Co, Ltd., Shenzhen, Guangdong
1st printing December 2017

Staff

Executive Committee
President: Jim O'Rourke
Vice President and Editor in Chief: Paul A. Kobasa
Vice President, Finance: Donald D. Keller
Vice President, Marketing: Jean Lin
Vice President, International Sales: Maksim Rutenberg
Vice President, Technology: Jason Dole
Director, Human Resources: Bev Ecker

Editorial
Director, New Print Publishing: Tom Evans
Senior Editor, New Print Publishing: Shawn Brennan
Writer: Mellonee Carrigan
Director, Digital Product Content Development: Emily Kline
Manager, Indexing Services: David Pofelski
Manager, Contracts & Compliance (Rights & Permissions): Loranne K. Shields
Librarian: S. Thomas Richardson

Digital
Director, Digital Product Development: Erika Meller
Digital Product Manager: Jonathan Wills

Graphics and Design
Senior Art Director: Tom Evans
Coordinator, Design Development and Production: Brenda Tropinski
Senior Visual Communications Designer: Melanie J. Bender
Media Researcher: Rosalia Bledsoe

Manufacturing/Pre-Press
Manufacturing Manager: Anne Fritzinger
Proofreader: Nathalie Strassheim

Photographic credits: Cover: © Gorodenkoff/Shutterstock; © iStockphoto: 7; Library of Congress: 27; Public Domain: 26; © Shutterstock: 4, 8, 10, 12, 15, 16, 18, 20, 22, 26, 27.

Illustrators: WORLD BOOK illustrations by Quadrum Ltd

What's inside?

This book tells you about some of the many important and interesting jobs that people do. What kind of work would you like to do when you grow up? This book may give you some ideas!

Accountant

An accountant is a person who helps people take care of money. Accountants help big and small businesses. They help families, too. They help the people who keep countries, towns, and cities going. Some accountants work in big accounting companies. Others work in small companies. Some own their own accounting business.

An accountant uses a **computer** to fill out financial **forms**.

Invoice

Num.	Qty	Units	Article Nr.	Goods, Service
1	1	pcs		Food photography for summer menu. Menu design and printin on glossy cardboard DIN A5 double sided 50 pieces
1	33	pcs.		Single product photo on white background
1	1	pcs.		Photo Licenses for Certifica

Total

Total Amount Payable

Some accountants help people fill out forms called income tax returns. People and companies need to tell the government how much money they make each year.

A **calculator** helps the accountant add up numbers.

Some accountants have a special **license**.

CERTIFICATE

It's a fact!
Accounting dates back to the earliest known civilizations of the Middle East and Central America. Skilled people called scribes did many of the accounting tasks.

Chef

Chefs work with food almost all day! Chefs are head cooks. They work in restaurants, hotels, cafeterias, and in homes. Chefs tell cooks and other kitchen workers what to do. They write recipes and plan menus. Chefs also help prepare and cook the food.

It's a fact!

Bon appetit!

Many French people think cooking is an art. Cooks all over the world have learned from French chefs for hundreds of years.

An **apron** protects a chef's clothing from food splashes and spills.

A chef uses a **thermometer** to make sure the food is the right temperature to serve.

Chefs usually wear a tall white hat called a **toque** (tohk).

Chefs arrange food with great care. They make each dish look beautiful.

A chef helps plan the **menu**. A menu is a list of foods in a meal.

Civil engineer

Civil engineers make plans for buildings, dams, bridges, highways, and railroads. Some civil engineers make plans for airports, pipelines, and water supply systems. Others study soil and rocks so buildings are put in the safest spots. Civil engineers usually work in offices or at construction sites. They tell the workers how to follow the plans.

Backhoes, cranes, and other big machines help do the work on a civil engineering project.

American civil engineer John Augustus Roebling was a pioneer in bridge building. He designed the Brooklyn Bridge in New York City, New York. It was built in 1883.

A civil engineer wears a **hardhat** to protect his head at a construction site—the spot where a building is going up.

A civil engineer reads a **blueprint**, a drawing that shows how to put up a building.

Dentist

A dentist is a doctor who helps us take care of our teeth. Dentists clean teeth and gums. They check for cavities (holes) in teeth. They fill the cavities to save the teeth and keep the mouth from hurting. Dentists also take out bad teeth. Dentists teach people how to care for their own teeth and gums.

It's a fact!

Stone Age people living in what is today the country of Pakistan used dental drills made of rock to remove tooth decay.

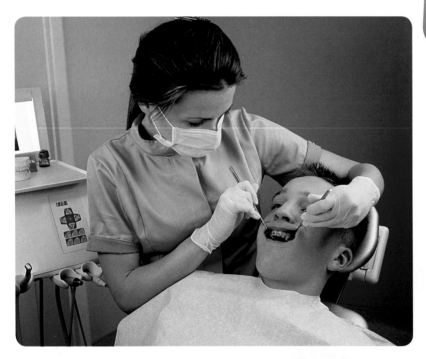

A **dental assistant** helps the dentist.

Gloves protect against the spread of germs.

An **orthodontist** is a special kind of dentist. Orthodontists put in **braces** to straighten crooked teeth. Small metal bands go around the teeth. Thin wires are fitted to the bands. Over time, the braces pull the teeth into the right places.

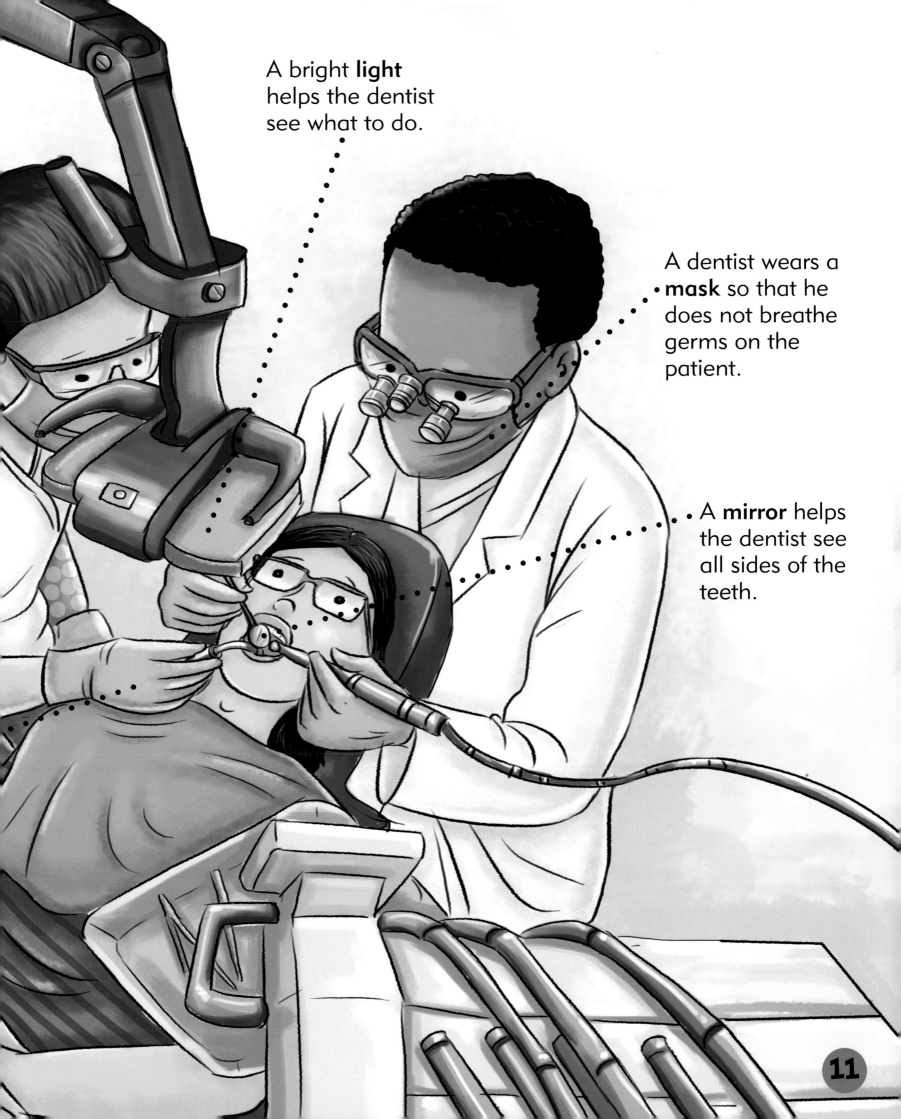

A bright **light** helps the dentist see what to do.

A dentist wears a **mask** so that he does not breathe germs on the patient.

A **mirror** helps the dentist see all sides of the teeth.

11

Electrical worker

Electrical workers set up and fix the power lines, wiring, and equipment that we use every day. Electric lights, television sets, computers, dishwashers, vacuum cleaners, and washing machines all need electric power to work. Electric power is made in buildings called power plants. Wires called power lines go from the plants to buildings and houses. The electric power comes to us on the power lines.

It's a fact!

Benjamin Franklin was one of the first people to experiment with electricity. In 1752, he described how he flew a homemade kite during a thunderstorm to prove that lightning is a giant electric spark.

An electrician must have more knowledge of electricity than an electrical worker. Electricians must understand architects' drawings and physics. Architects are people who design buildings. Physics is the study of matter (what things are made of) and energy.

Rubber gloves and **rubber-soled shoes** protect the electrical worker from getting shocked by an electric current.

An electrical worker fixes a **power line.**

A **hardhat** protects the electrical worker's head in case of a fall.

Safety glasses protect the eyes.

An electrical worker attaches herself to the pole with a **belt** so that she does not fall.

Farmer

A farmer is a person who grows crops (plants) or raises animals for food on a farm. Farmers grow nearly all of the food that we eat. Farmers and other farmworkers spend a lot of time working outdoors. The weather is a big part of having a good or poor harvest.

Chopped plants and other things for farm animals to eat are kept in a building called a **silo**.

Farmers plant **crops** and harvest (pick) them when they are ready.

Farmers feed and take care of **livestock** (farm animals).

Hay for livestock to eat is kept dry in a **barn**.

Farmworkers run many kinds of farm machines. **Tractors** are one of the most important machines on most farms.

Lawyer

A lawyer, or attorney, is a person who tells people what the laws are and helps people use the laws. Some lawyers try to help people who may have broken a law. Other lawyers try to show that someone did break a law. And other lawyers write papers to help people do business with each other or take care of what they own.

A lawyer speaks in a **courtroom** (room for trials).

A **judge** is in charge of the court.

People who want to be a lawyer must learn the law and pass a special test called a bar exam.

A lawyer's **client** may be a person or a company.

It's a fact!

British judges and barristers (lawyers) wear wigs and robes in the courtroom.

A group of people called a **jury** listens to the case.

A **lawyer** presents her client's case.

Plumber

Plumbers help us get clean and stay warm in many ways. A plumber puts in or fixes pipes that carry water into and out of buildings. Plumbers put in and fix sinks, toilets, bathtubs, boilers, and showers. They stop leaks and unclog drains. Plumbers also connect dishwashers and washing machines to the water pipes in a house.

The plumber works on pipes below the **sink**.

A plumber uses a special **tool** to unclog a drain.

When people turn on a **faucet,** a valve opens and lets the water flow in.

A **pipe** carries water into and out of a building.

Scientist

Scientists study why and how things happen. They try to learn about the world, especially about nature. Scientists study many different subjects. Some scientists study how plants and animals live and grow. Some study Earth. Others study the universe and the things in it.

A scientist who studies living things is called a **biologist**.

A clean **lab coat** protects against spills in the lab.

Zoologists study how animals live. The zoologists learn what can help or hurt animals.

It's a fact!

Mathematics and medicine were the first sciences.

Special glasses called **goggles** keep scientists' eyes safe in the lab.

•A **microscope** makes tiny things look bigger.

This scientist works in a **laboratory**, a special place to do scientific experiments and investigations.

21

Software engineer

Software engineers write the instructions (rules) that computers follow. These instructions are called a software program. The program tells a computer what to do and how to do it. Software programs help people do different kinds of work on the computer. Software works together with hardware, the parts of a computer you can touch.

Some software engineers create games that can be played on a computer.

A software engineer writes a program in a **code** (computer language).

A computer's hardware includes the **keyboard** and **screen**.

A software engineer uses a **computer** to create electronic instructions.

Career Day

Career Day is a special day at many schools. Students can meet people from their community who can tell them about different jobs and careers. Students can find out about the kinds of work they would like to do and ask questions.

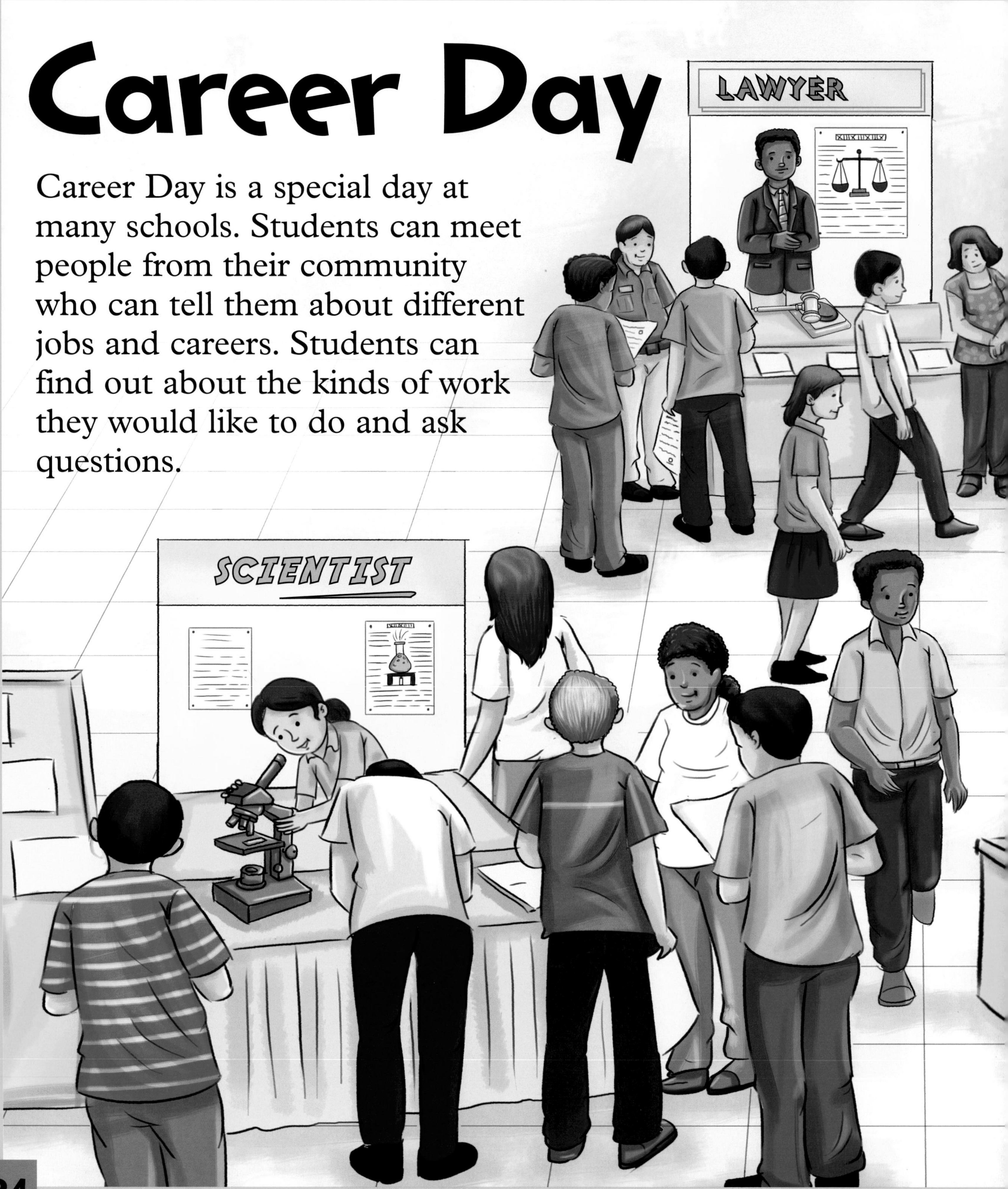

LAWYER

SCIENTIST

Which job works with teeth?

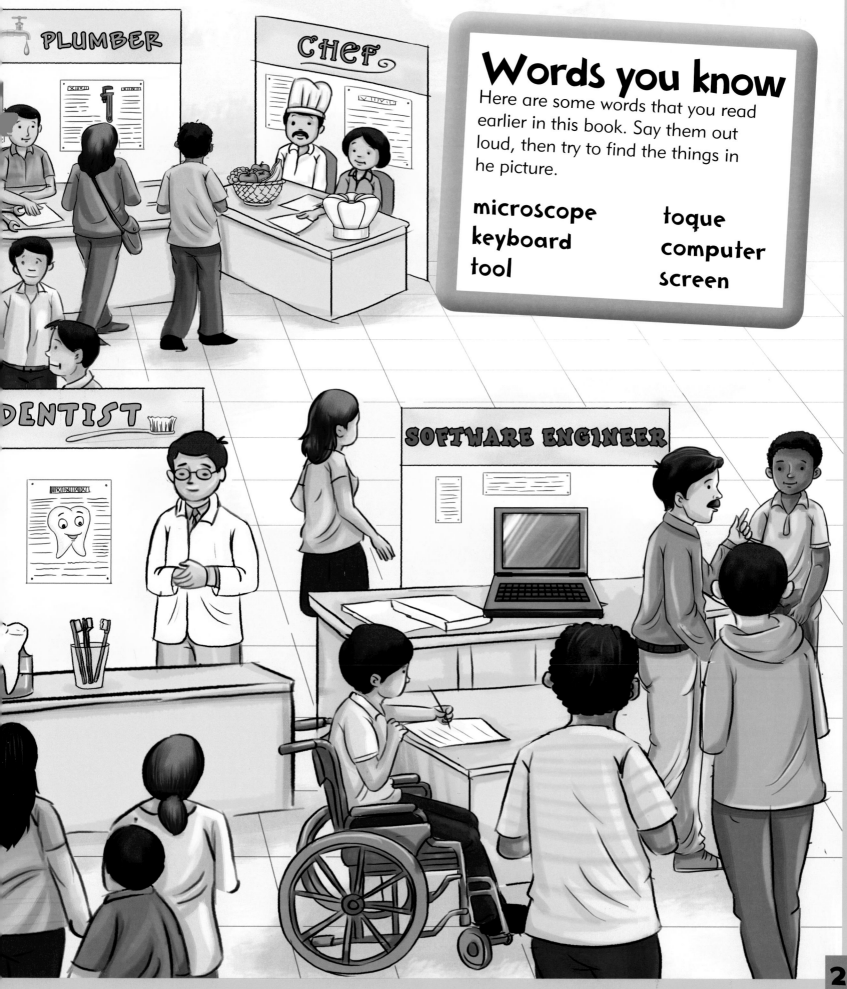

Words you know

Here are some words that you read earlier in this book. Say them out loud, then try to find the things in he picture.

microscope
keyboard
tool

toque
computer
screen

PLUMBER

CHEF

DENTIST

SOFTWARE ENGINEER

In which job do you wear a special hat?

Did you know?

Many chefs learn to cook at the Cordon Bleu, a famous school of French cooking in Paris, France.

From the 400's to the 1400's, dentistry was often done by jewelers and barbers. Ouch!

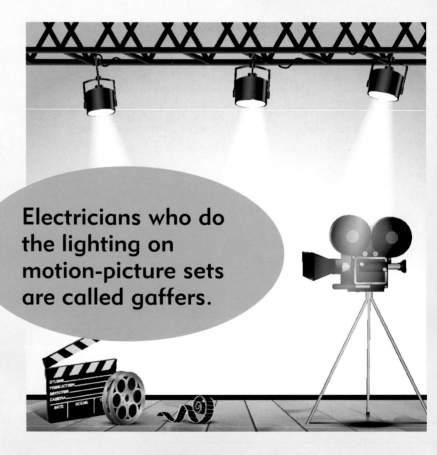

Electricians who do the lighting on motion-picture sets are called gaffers.

In some countries, half or more of the people still work as farmers.

About three-fifths of all the presidents of the United States have been lawyers.

The American software engineer Jack Dorsey came up with the idea for the social networking website Twitter in 2006.

Puzzles

Close-up!

We've zoomed in on three people who work in different jobs. Can you figure out which job each person has?

Answers on page 32.

Double trouble!

These two pictures are not exactly the same. Find the six things that are different in picture b.

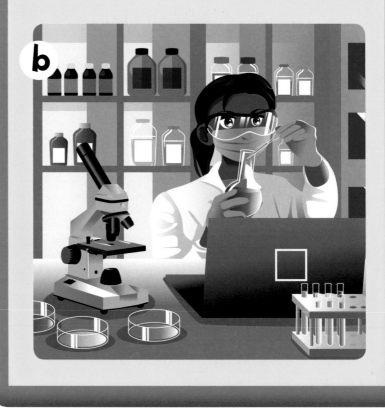

Match up!

Match each word on the left with its picture on the right.

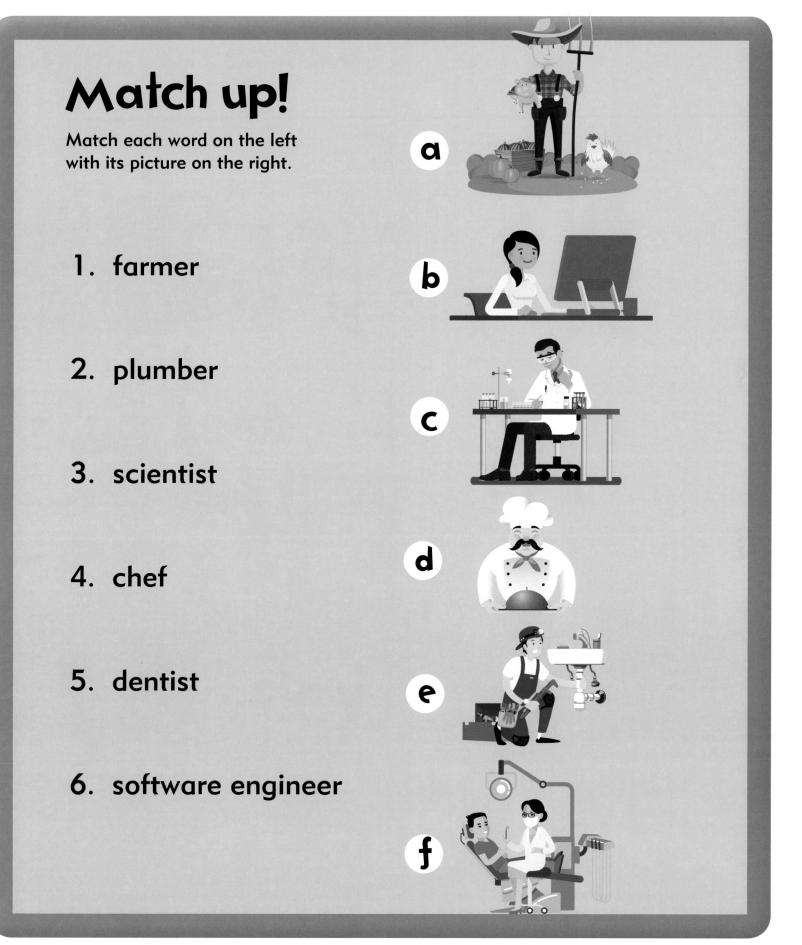

1. farmer

2. plumber

3. scientist

4. chef

5. dentist

6. software engineer

a
b
c
d
e
f

Answers on page 32.

True or false

Can you figure out which of these statements are true? Go to the page numbers given to help you find the answers.

3 Dentists teach people how to care for their own teeth and gums. **Go to page 10.**

1 Chefs only work in restaurants. **Go to page 6.**

4 A biologist studies living things. **Go to page 20.**

2 Software engineers build airports, bridges, highways, and railroads. **Go to page 22.**

5 More than half of the world's people are farmers. **Go to page 15.**

Answers on page 32.

Find out more

Books

Be What You Want by J. M. Bedell and others (Aladdin/Beyond Words, 2012-2017). Ten volumes. Each book, including *So You Want to Work in Fashion* and *So You Want to Be a Dancer*, explains what the field is like and how to prepare for a career in that field.

Cool Vocational Careers by Ellen Labrecque (Cherry Lake, 2017). Eight volumes. These books describe careers that don't require a four-year college degree, such as auto technician and commercial fisher.

Hooray for Community Helpers! by Elle Parkes and Kurt Waldendorf (Bumba Books, 2017). Eight volumes.
This series includes *Hooray for Teachers!, Hooray for Farmers!, Hooray for Veterinarians!* and others. Each book describes how a person in that job serves his or her community.

When I Grow Up by Connie Colwell Miller (Amicus Publishing, 2017). Six volumes.
I'll Be a Musician and *I'll Be a Chef* are two of the books in this series that shows children pretending to have these careers.

Websites

Jobs and Careers
https://kids.usa.gov/jobs/index.shtml
This U.S. government website offers text, video, and interviews with people in a variety of careers, such as dentistry, aviation, and law enforcement.

Know It All.org
https://www.knowitall.org/subject/career-education
People in many jobs, from accountant to actor, discuss in videos what they do. From the state of South Carolina.

Smithsonian Institution
http://insider.si.edu/category/meet-our-scientists/
Explore science careers by learning about what the famed Smithsonian's scientists do.

United States Bureau of Labor Statistics
https://www.bls.gov/k12/
This resource for students and teachers can help kids find careers and learn about the U.S. economy.

Answers

Puzzles
from pages 28 and 29

Close-up!
1. chef
2. dentist
3. plumber

Double trouble!
In picture b, the four pill bottles on the shelf have been replaced with two blue-green bottles, the microscope has changed position, the flask the scientist is holding is a different shape, the liquid in the flask is a different color, the oval shape on the computer cover changed to a square, and there are more test tubes.

Match up!
1. a   2. e   3. c
4. d   5. f   6. b

True or false
from page 30

1. false   2. false
3. true   4. true
5. false

Index